Advance praise

Wild Grace

"Chelan Harkin's latest compilation of mystic poetry extracts pearls from the depths of despair, with the fearless fortitude of a world-class free diver. As a seasoned sherpa, she leads readers by the hand and heart through the valley of ego death with occasional paroxysms of 'hooting and hollering.' With equal parts tenderness and ferocity, *Wild Grace* adds a generous dollop of the Divine Feminine and a singular poeticism to a spiritual travel guide that should find its soon-to-be coffee-stained and dogeared way into the backpacks of many a soul sojourner." —**Nipun Mehta, Founder of ServiceSpace**

"*Wild Grace* is Chelan Harkin's most moving collection of poetry yet. Each poem is a satisfying dish, chock-full of fresh insights and earned epiphanies—and spiced with a dash of humor. In our overscheduled, too-busy lives, Harkin reminds us that we are, at heart, spiritual beings. These poems are deeply nourishing. It's impossible to read them without feeling something long dormant stir inside you." —**Eric Weiner, *New York Times* Best-selling author of *The Geography of Bliss* and *The Geography of Genius***

"There's a Vedic saying: 'Thy gifts, my Lord, I surrender to Thee.' Chelan has indeed received a Divine gift. I don't think ordinary human intelligence could express such depth in words. She is an instrument of the Divine. We all are, to varying degrees and in various ways. But rarely are our expressions so sublime and uplifting as hers. And she's so young! I think that centuries from now, people will still be inspired by her poetry." —**Rick Archer, host of podcast Buddha at the Gas Pump: Conversations with "Ordinary" Spiritually Awakening People**

Praise for

"Hafiz says, 'God and I have become like two giant fat people living in a tiny boat. We keep bumping into each other and laughing.' May this collection help you feel the possibility of that kind of laughter." —**Daniel Ladinsky,** *The Gift*

"In her writing and in her life, Chelan has two goals: to bring acceptance, belonging, and worth to all of those uncomfortable emotions we've been taught to hate; and to make room for our hearts in a heady world." —*Spiritual Wanderlust with Kelly Deutsch* **(podcast)**

"These pages bear witness to a beautifully reckless and vulnerable love. *Susceptible to Light* shares the ineffable, all-consuming love of a Rumi or Hafiz, but situated in the here-and-now, amidst our dirty dishes and carpools. Do yourself a favor and savor these poems." —**Eric Weiner, bestselling author of books such as** *The Geography of Bliss* **and, most recently,** *The Socrates Express*

"This is a beautiful compilation of WOWS! Let yourself be carried away on this ecstatic current of wonder-drenched poems and you will surely find your heart singing and dancing with each and every beautiful offering." —**Tina M. Benson, M.A., international bestselling author of** *A Woman unto Herself*

"All your tears will find sisters in her poems, and all your laughter will find a home in her belly. Her poems are just plain fun to read, yet they take us to the deepest darkest loam, where lightning goes." —**Alfred K. LaMotte, author of** *Wounded Bud*

"University press-published poets would love to reach as many readers as Chelan Harkin is finding. Her poems are visionary, mystical, and contemplative. Her teaching is from the perennial wisdom of all the great religious and spiritual traditions, where the final goal of all existence is union, and that is divine." —*SpiritualityandPractice.com*

"Inspired poetry has been flowing through Chelan Harkin for years though her publishing journey is just a little less than two years old. Her launch into sharing her poetry with the world has been mystical, transformational and filled with prayer experiments gone right."
—*What Matters Most with Paul Samuel Dolman* (podcast)

"In her poetry and in life, Chelan continually invites the fumbling, suffering parts of ourselves and our divine nature to meet for tea in the heart, to have a great laugh in the belly, and share a big hug." —**Mark Peters, "Awakin Call" at Dailygood.org**

"The palpable sway of God in Chelan's poetry reminds us that she is one of few women in history to earn a seat at the sacred table of authentic mystic poets. She writes with a holy force that hurls us past the predictable civil tones of standard spiritual poetry and straight into an intoxicating celebration of truths so pure our spirit can't help but stagger drunkenly in resonance." —**Mary Reed, author of *Unwitting Mystic***

Wild Grace

POEMS

CHELAN HARKIN

Monkfish Book Publishing Company
Rhinebeck, New York

Paperback ISBN 978-1-958972-12-0
eBook ISBN 978-1-958972-13-7

Library of Congress Cataloging-in-Publication Data

Names: Harkin, Chelan, author.
Title: Wild grace : poems / Chelan Harkin.
Other titles: Wild grace (Compilation)
Description: Rhinebeck, New York : Monkfish Book Publishing Company, [2023]
Identifiers: LCCN 2023020344 (print) | LCCN 2023020345 (ebook) | ISBN 9781958972120 (paperback) | ISBN 9781958972137 (ebook)
Subjects: LCGFT: Poetry.
Classification: LCC PS3608.A7424 W55 2023 (print) | LCC PS3608.A7424 (ebook) | DDC 811/.6--dc23/eng/20230518
LC record available at https://lccn.loc.gov/2023020344
LC ebook record available at https://lccn.loc.gov/2023020345

Book and cover design by Colin Rolfe

Monkfish Book Publishing Company
22 East Market Street, Suite 304
Rhinebeck, New York 12572
(845) 876-4861
monkfishpublishing.com

CONTENTS

GOD KISSED THE DEVIL

When I opened my heart
I caught God
kissing the devil

right there in the bedchambers
of my chest.

It was quite the scandal
and pretty much toppled everything.

Right and Wrong were like, "Woah!
We can do that?!"
And rushed into each other's arms.

The affection that began
between Good and Bad
would have been fiercely scorned
by most of the angels
had they been living
by the stringent doctrines of their past.

But they'd already stripped naked
and started running
through my whole body,
hooting and hollering
and causing a holy ruckus
of pure aliveness.

In that moment,
every evil touched
its original innocence.

And I could no longer be bothered
investing my life
in the deadening work of judgement.

CRUSHED INTO WINE

As a grape ripens
until it is ready
to be crushed
into wine,

So too does your pain
ripen within you
until it is ready
to be crushed
into love.

It's when we forget
the destiny of all hearts
is Love's Great Barrel
that suffering takes
such great hold.

The missing ingredient
for peace
as you ripen
toward Love's obliteration
of complete becoming,
is trust
in The Vintner's
sacred timing.

RUMI'S HEART

Rumi's heart,
more than an orb
of unattainable light
set above you,

was more likely
a hopelessly unfixable
broken pot

through which light
was merciful enough
to continually spill.

Hafez, most likely,
was a gardener
of sorrow—
he knew how to bring its aching
to blossom, and open you
to beauty there.

I'm sorry if this disappoints you,
that even the greats
aren't elitist untouchables
that have defied suffering.

Even Jesus, Muhammad, The Buddha—
all those Great Ones—
must have held tenderly
in their own chests
the deepest ravines of humanity's sorrow—
how else could they have known
compassion like that?

They simply knew
how to kneel down deep enough
to kiss that wound.

Don't do that unnatural thing
of separating the sacred
from its sorrow.

Artists of the deep heart
are not apart from suffering.
They've learned the craft
of melting it into gold.

They don't flee from fire—
they make it their medium.

I'VE NEVER READ THE BIBLE

I've never read the Bible.
I don't know the difference
between Exodus and Genesis.

I can't distinguish between the heart
of what's said in the New Testament, the Old Testament
or the Quran.

Scripture all just looks like arrows
pointing in.

But I can tell you what it feels like
when God crawls up my spine

or when She lights a fire in my heart
to warm Herself.

I know the pound of Her gavel
when She says "No" in my gut.

Or when Her "Yes" pops a cork in my soul
and She drinks and drinks.

My poetry is what happens
when She whispers to me

and Her lullaby
is my deepening breath
as She rocks me to sleep.

She's known to be found
lulling in the siesta of each
of my fat cells

or strength training
in my voice box
to add more weight
to my truth.

She is what makes the night bearable.
She is what draws me toward each morning.

Don't just take Her word for it
with scripture.

Dive into Her limitlessness
inside you
now—

She wants you to know Yourself.

CONSERVATIVE ESTIMATE

They say there's a 1 in 30 trillion chance
of you existing at all...

but I think that's a conservative estimate.

When you factor in
that a universe
happened to explode
from something the size of a marble,
or a pin prick,
we immediately move beyond incalculability.

And adding the unlikelihood
that the destruction of that blast
would have created
a vast city of stars
with a place tucked into it
called Earth
that would be soft and fertile enough
to accommodate the holy and mysterious concept
of *mother*,
the odds become wilder yet.

Or think about how the waves
of this mighty thing
we've come to call the sea

had some great tidal moment
that washed your sea-born, squid-like
prehistoric ancestors
into each other's arms or tentacles or fins
to procreate the possibility *of you*.

Or consider all the phenomena that led
a later ancestor out of his cave
to follow a trail of pheromones
toward your hairy
very great, great grandmother
to grunt at her in some alluring way

Or simply that your mother
held a magical jewel inside of her
that carried half of the potential
of your DNA,
which is just scientific jargon for,
The Scripture of You,
and that a magnetic force called love is here
that pulled your father toward her.

What is the equation
for water existing
to quench your longing for it?

Or that an asteroid crashed
into the dinosaurs
at just the right moment
to give mammals the possibility of ascendance?

Or that each ice age froze
and thawed time
just so
to create the propitious conditions
for life's waters
to flow in your direction?

How might we sum up the truth
that you would not be here
were it not for every other luminous
pulse and beat and swell

of this magnificent, wonder drenched
system of stars and death and wombs
and the great explosion
of life?

What exponents would suffice
to express that every minute and magnificent happening
throughout the eternity of beginning-less time
has necessitated your life?

There is no number we could give
that could equal the astronomical mystery
of life's grand total
of you.

You are unbelievable—
as unlikely as God.

Dear one, we just have to round it all up
to miracle.

HONOR THE EARTH

I want to honor the Earth
for Her truthfulness.

She doesn't slap a smile
over Her thunder

Or say, "calm down"
to Her storms.

She can't for long
hold back the depth of feeling
inside Her clouds—

She honors herself enough
to rain whenever and wherever
She goddamn pleases
with no consideration for convenience
until She's satisfied.

The latent periods of Her volcano's fire,
Her belly's cauldron,
are always temporary.

Her wisdom
has its own timing.

And She never apologizes
for Her overcast skies—
why would she?

Her winters
get just as much stage time
as Her springs.

And from Her trees
She routinely relinquishes
everything that's gotten them attention
each year.

She almost seems to enjoy
the gnarly look
of the snag,

or the black arrow of birds
cutting through the thick,
gray wool clouds of Her impenetrable skies.

She is at ease
in Her darkness.
Blue skies come on Her terms.

She does not appease you
by being warm all the time
or pleasant.

At times She is blisteringly harsh
to test your resilience.

She is a wild canopy
of the living and dying—

as much breakdown
as blossom.

TOTAL BREAKDOWN

"She's having a total breakdown,"
one put together
and very self-satisfied seed
with no cracks in it
whispered to another
about a third seed who had begun
to germinate.

"She's completely falling apart—
her life is a mess!"

They gazed superiorly
at the smooth, intact facade
of their shells
so perfectly upholding
expectations of the status quo.

Clearly, compared to that wild,
sprouting seed
disrupting the peace,
they were doing something right…right?

But now and then,
they secretly looked up
with longing at the tall-stemmed,
bravely opened flower
wondering if there might be
more to themselves.

PERMISSION TO SAY ANYTHING

The world needs your voice.

Dig deep into your latent magma
and erupt your sorrow onto the page.

Step out of the robe of your facade
and show your truth to us trembling.

Whatever your writer's block
dip your pen into the heart of its reasons
and tell about that—

about the flat lands
with no topography of inspiration
you've been wandering down
for so long.

About how Muse seems
an endangered species—

let us feel your drought of God.

Tell us about the curvature
of the ice block of your numbness
and all the factors
that have carved its shape.

Tell us of your affairs
with loneliness
and how you can't seem to stop returning
to her cold bed.

Talk about the writers you're jealous of
how all you want to do is sign your name
to their flame.

Invite us into the catacombs of your fears.

Show us the graveyards in your heart
filled with all the beloved things
you've lost.

Don't just give us pictures
of the bathed, swaddled baby,
the tidy aftermath.

We want to know the pangs
of how you've birthed yourself
or aborted this process
time and time again.

Yearning is the siren
that summons the writer—
sing us her song.

The world needs your voice.
Un-sheath your knowing.
You have permission
to say anything.

HOW TO WRITE INSPIRED POETRY

Let yourself be ugly,
a wild hag howling at nighttime
unsure if the morning will ever come.

Give yourself permission to dip your pen
into the golden ink
in the center of the sun,
as well as the winter solstice
of your darkest sorrow.

Make an outlaw of your pen
bold enough
to unlock
your oldest prisoners.

Bring forth the repressed passion
in the center of your fire
and make a great conflagration
of your desire.

Say whatever has long been
in your heart
that your parents
couldn't hear.

Do whatever you can
to make God laugh,
and try to describe that Great Sound
that every other noise in this world
is desperately trying to plagiarize.

Go to the bedside of each
unresolved heartache
and inscribe its last words.

Pass agony the mic
and watch tenderness
uncurl from her
as she's allowed to tell
her full story.

Poetry is where the flint of soul
strikes the stone of trauma
and makes a spark.

FULLY HUMAN

Comedians need a space to cry,

and spiritual leaders need a space
to share their insecurities
and how vulnerable they feel.

Religious people need a space
to share their doubts,

and priests need a space to confess
their desires.

Mothers need a space to wail
about how regularly
we long to escape motherhood,

and parents need permission
to curl their hurts into fetal position
and cradle their hearts.

It must be okay for saints
to also have scuff marks,

and for the monk to long
to come down from the mountaintop.

And mystics must be allowed
to trudge
through the mundane.

To stay in honest and whole relationship
we need to be able to tell God
we hate Him
now and then.

For our light
to go on sustaining itself
it must be allowed its shadow.

AWAKENING IS MESSY

Awakening is messy.

You don't transcend
into some paradisiacal,
elitist inner garden—

It doesn't perfect you.

You first come into
all the reasons you've so wanted
to stay asleep.

And there are many
good reasons.

To awaken, really,
is to begin to feel.

Awakening is bit by bit
coming out of denial
around all the reasons you've needed
to wield
that terrible tool of othering—
because so much is unbearable
inside of our own self.

It is diving into the cracks
in our hearts
rather than mortaring them.
It does not look like being
perfectly empowered,
seamlessly composed—

It's to commit with all your heart
to no longer take out your helplessness
on anyone else.

Awakening has nothing to do
with stern, stoic spirituality.
It has nothing to do
with finally being aloof enough
to not be impacted by the gifts
of your feelings.

Awakening doesn't come
from spiritual mastery defined
as overcoming enough of our shortcomings.

It is found in doing our fumbling best
to grow into arms strong and loving enough
to hold and hug our aching humanity.

The myth that awakening
looks anything like spiritual perfectionism
is perhaps the best sleeping pill.

Awakening is the at times compass-less
and often inglorious
inner odyssey
toward the rough ruby of all that is bruised
and true in our hearts.

Awakening isn't only for special people.
We're all on our way
toward coming out of the sleep cycle.

PIERCE YOUR PRIDE

Let the sword
that pierces your pride
cut deep,

and trace its blade
in and down
to the most humble wound
that has too long been defended
by your reactions.

Stay there
as you weep out the poison
of hiding.

Stay there and experience
transformation
as your deepest shames,
given to light,
become flags of honor
in the great victory
of no longer having
to reject yourself.

It is in that heroic lack
of hiding your hurt
that you let grace
into your heart.

You are changing the world
through changing your patterns.

Feel your pain
all the way through
to the point where it blooms
forgiveness.

You are remaking the past now
with your courage
to no longer ferment pain
into an arsenal.

You are melting those guns
into shovels,
and with them,
you are turning the soil
that will grow a new world.

BE A HERETIC

Shed the skins
of every old God
in your mind.

Be a heretic
if being a heretic means
abandoning
the increasingly empty reward
of how closely you can follow
other people's rules.

There is a fine and devastating
untangling
of comfortable falsity
your soul must go through
to become anew.

Ask any question that frees you
from old ways
made for the long dead.

Liberate yourself
from the sarcophagus
of a role
that casts a statue
of your whirling soul.

SHADOW SHERPA

With my pen I gut the heavens
and spill luminous entrails
all over the earth—

let the soul hungry hounds lap it up.

I graft God to people's
deepest wounds
and suture spirit to the ordinary.

I brail the stars
feeling for the secret code
to unlock every nighttime
from your heart.

A poet is a thief of light
robbing beauty-rich places.

I plunder morning
for all her golden coins
and scatter them
across my page
for you to collect.

I scour your darkness looking
for tracks of God.

My verse is a shadow sherpa
guiding you down the steepest slopes
of your sorrow—

I look the glorious future in the eye
and turn us that way.

IF GOD IS ANYTHING

I am certain
that if God is anything,
She is a great lover of science,
the genius behind the motivation
to make quarks and nuclear fusion,
elemental reactions and orbits.

I am certain
that if God is anything,
She is a wild painter with ADHD
who will not stop Her creative impulses
to pour Her muse over all existence
to tend to trivial matters.

I am certain
that if God is anything,
She is an eccentric inventor
who designed the religions
to kiss each other—
for Christianity and Islam
to run off together
like two wild lovers in the night.

I am certain
that if God is anything,
She is a child
that has not for an instant
been interested in wrath.

And whose single commandment
is to eternally celebrate
your original innocence.

WE DRINK THE SAME WATER

We drink the same water
that dinosaurs drank,

that Muhammad used
for his ablutions,

that Jesus used
to wash his disciples' feet,

that our ancestors emerged from
to try legs,

the same water that crashes
in a quintessence
of creation's power
at the base
of Niagra Falls.

We drink the same water
that has lived inside each other's tears—
some deep part of us
has tasted the suffering of all,
and the tenderness.

Our bodies are made of tributaries,
oceans and clouds,
we cycle through each other.

We are the unconditional baptism
of rain—
the heavens have always known
the whole earth is holy.

We are Everest's mists,

we are the evaporation
from The Amazon,

we are the atmosphere.

We are made of ancient water
and our makeup is continually recycled
through the heavens.

IT'S NOT SO MUCH THAT I WANT
TO KNOW GOD

It's not so much that I want
to know God

As to be close to the spiral
in the seashell,

To feel the wind
as my own breath,

To let birdsong all the way in
to my being,
let my bones
be the ledger lines
for its song.

It's not so much
that I want to know God

as to be reacquainted
with the intimacies of the stars
through remembering
they've always shone from within
the expansiveness of my own chest.

It's not so much that I want
to please any Cosmic Authority
as to be strong enough
for the little girl still inside of me
to feel held and finally able
to weep old tears.

It's not so much that I need a particular
place of worship—

I want to abide
in the majesty of each moment

that the humble door
of my ancient heart
be more willing to open
to the wide beauty
of the world.

My only prayer is to be excommunicated
from idealogy
and feel divine guidance
coursing through me.

It's not so much
that I want to worship God
as to remember
to say thank you
with deep recognition
for every small act of love
that finds me.

I care not to serve an abstract God.
My only desire is to serve
the One Great Heart
that lives within us all.

ASTONISHMENT

A prerequisite of poetry
is the in-breath of astonishment
for exactly what is—
and don't make this hard for yourself.

Astonishment is the secret
within every ordinary thing.

You needn't make the flower
uncomfortable
by forcing her into a stare off
for several hours
intimidating her into telling you
her secrets—
Grace is dulled by this.

You needn't interrogate
the moon
demanding that she spit out strings
of pearlescent stanzas.

And you don't need to pretzel your body
into a meditation or yoga position
that makes it whimper
and force it to stay.

You needn't push your edge-less heart
to conform to any hard mold

or try so hard
to squeeze color from the sunset
onto your page
like a vibrant, cosmic pimple.

You needn't work so hard
to extract beauty from yourself
or this soft,
generous world.

Just notice how things are,
the grace of the way
things have landed in your life:
Savor your coffee, notice the clutter
of the things on your shelf—
that collection of tidbits
from the peculiar gift
of your only life.

And from that place—
not manicured or controlled
but loose haired and uniquely yours—
just start saying something about it.

Walk into the woods,
lay your thanks upon everything
like sunlight,
and poetry, that beauty creature,
will emerge and approach you.

WILD GRACE

Put me amidst life's
simplest things

that give their lives to blooming
or quietly glowing
without reaching for a name.

Open me in a way
that allows silence
to be a deep source of nourishment.

Let me gather the great bundle
of my every mistake and shortcoming
into my arms like a vast bouquet
and thank it for making
a gentler and more honest place
out of my heart.

I want no spiritual mastery,
but to be porous like the earth
to the nourishing rain.

Dear God, if you please,
no more of this distance.
Plant yourself in my body.

I want nothing
but to be alive
with Wild Grace.

COMMANDMENTS OF JOY

Your children want you
with a sacred fervor.

They don't want to admire
some prettied-up shell of you
that you show to the public.

They want to drudge up your heart
out of the conditioned nonsense
of serious occupations
and persuade you
to collect the stars
in your skirts,
berry stain the cheeks
of your life
and come to remember
your original joy.

Children are your life's
great revolutionaries
if you let them be.

They tear you
with their tenderness
from the arms of distraction
so that you might
be fully able to hold them.

They don't care
if you're rich, smart, beautiful, thin
and they're marvelously disinterested
in your external success.

They want you to crouch down
on all fours and invite you
to burrow into sacred aliveness
with them.

They invite you to let go
of your doctrine
of perfectionism
and behold the sacred mess
of this moment.

Your kids do not want you
to worship the God of fear—

they want you to believe
in the God
who would want you
to put extra whipped cream
on things.

Oh, let them
re-write scripture
in scrawled crayon
that lists only commandments
of joy.

GOD'S TASTING ROOM

Eat a piece of heavily buttered
homemade bread
with devotional grade satisfaction.

Kiss somebody.

Put your naked body
in mineral springs,
the warm baths
Mother Nature has drawn for you.

Cook your grandmother's
favorite meal
while shaking your hips
to her favorite tune.

Touch the earth,
star bathe.

As often as you can
take the holy sacrament
of homemade pie-—
let your tastebuds give great thanks.

Celebrate the holy hell
out of your glorious materiality.

This earth is God's tasting room.
Let each of your senses
be Her honored host.

TINY SPROUT

What would happen
if we could be as satisfied
by the tiny sprout
emerging from the ground
as we are about a big promotion?

As infatuated
with the newly opened daffodil
as we might be with a new lover?

What if we tuned in
to the detail of a leaf,
or the mood of the forest
after a rain
as closely as we notice
our own shortcomings?

How do we re-sensitize our hearts
to feel the love
poured upon the world
from the blush of each sunset?

How do we prioritize
our gratitude
so that instead of consuming
the whole earth
in a way that will never fill us,
a single dew drop
could satisfy our thirsts?

Every part of us is an antenna for beauty,
a receptor for divine tenderness.

What might it be like
if we could take the hierarchy
out of experience?

And practiced being so replete
with sacred wonder,
so quenched with recognition
that nothing about ourselves
requires even a drop
of enhancement?

LUSCIOUS DARKNESS

I've arrived!"
said the full moon.

"I've figured it out!
I'll stay whole this time.
I won't wane anymore.
No more darkness!"

And hasn't your heart
thought the same thing
right before another plunge
into its necessary school
of shadows?

To insist on staying light
is unnatural
and without elegance.

Darling, embrace the rhythm
of descent
into your darkness.

THE HOLY WORD *"SHE"*

I don't think God has a vagina
or has ever had a penis.

But to use that holy word, *"She"*
to describe the divine
is the sweetest shorthand
to overturn everything.

She is gloriously subversive.
She is radical—
meaning essential, of the roots.

Rather than up and out,
She brings us down
and in.

She brings us into the fertile lands
of our bodies,
into the intersection
of ancient wounds and wisdoms.

She is what motivates our untold stories
into their telling.

She is what germinates truth.

She speaks of a God that understands Mothers.

She undoes a power-over paradigm
and describes power that comes from a cracked
open heart.

She knows feeling
is essential to reverence.

She restores tears
to worship.

She honors pain as much as purity,
the sullied as much as the sanctified

She is the vastness of oceans,
She is the soft fire
of the moon.

She
is the revolution
birthing in our hearts.

THE HOLY WORD "NO"

This one is for any woman
in my ancestral line
for whom the primordial form
of the holy word, "No"
began forming in her gut,
in her root,
in the deepest furrows
of her knowing—

that it would become the torch
of justice and discernment
that would one day
be passed down
to me.

BENEATH MY ANGER

Beneath my anger
that wants to itemize
your shortcomings
so you can see
and undo
all the ways I've let you
hurt me

are my inadequacies,
my beliefs
that another's limitations
on how to love
have the power
to devalue me.

But another's whims
can never
determine my worth.

So it is here,
in the brutal accountability
of all still unresolved
inside myself,
that I must stay

As I reclaim my power
by taking back
the full measure of my pain.

ALCHEMICAL RAGE

If I am to love you
with any kind
of full breath

then I need to tell you
about my rage—

about the fire
in my belly
that wants to bring forth
all the needs
I haven't listened to.

If you are to see me
in anything close
to my full power,
you need to see me
in my rage.

If you are to see me
in anything close
to my full beauty,
I need to tell you
about my rage.

Rage does not have
to be violent.
Primarily it is a conversation
between the self
and the self
about coming out of denial

and coronating
the once condemned.

Rage does not have to be destructive.
It can put the full power
of life
back together again
by reclaiming what has been lost.

It is the brawn that brings up
the long buried.

It is plunging in
to the hemmed
and edited self
to pull forth the raw
and the real.

It rolls the boulder off of our silence.
It empowers the voice
that was once too vulnerable.

It does not need
to come from blame
or projection.
It is a super-power
stronger
than self-rejection.

It says,
"I'm not equanimous about this.
No more of this c'est la vie bullshit
that hides my hurt—
this matters."

Rage is recognition.
Rage is a love language
of life
for my entirety.
Rage is wildly in love
with my wholeness.

LOOK OUT FOR THAT ONE

"Look out for that one,"

They said of the woman
who didn't move within the lines.

"She's becoming free."

"What do you mean, free?"
a little girl asked, attracted, intrigued.

"She sees what she sees and she speaks it—
and she's breaking
the last boundary
in caring less
what men think of her.

Somehow, un-ensnaring herself
from the million commandments
She must abide by to please
the patriarchy,

She seems to be finding
a deep well within,
and is able to source
her own happiness.

Stay away from her.
She is dangerous.
The status quo un-tames itself
around her.

She is a clear blade
of justice.

She is becoming
one of those destructive ones
who whirls
while the old world
crumbles down.

There is no way to contain her!

She's as ravenous for her shadows
as she is her light.

She is not afraid
of the dark."

The little girl sat watching
wide-eyed and said,

"Do you think
she could teach me
how to dance?"

I AM BEAUTIFUL

I am beautiful!

And this beauty is not
a comparative thing.

It is a realization,
a claiming.

It has nothing to do
with being more or less
beautiful than you.
It is not about proving anything.

It comes
from the ability
to see rightly.

To know your beauty
is to become a mountain
rooted and secure
in your substance.

I am beautiful
because I have bathed
in the unwilting light
of all that I am.

I am beautiful
because I have found
within me
a ceaseless song,

and my DNA is laced
with moonlight.

I am beautiful
because I have wiped
all the makeup
off the face of God.

My soul
has adorned itself
with a light
that needs no enhancement.

A PATH BACK TO MYSELF

The path back to myself
has been the perpetual passage
through the dark doors

of sorrow
that so guard
my heart.

I enter
when I can no longer bear
my longing for myself.

WILLING TO WEEP

This is a poem
for those who are healing
their trauma.

I'm not just speaking
of those traumas
with a capital T—

but of any wound
too frozen
to weep.

There are a million ways
we learn to leave ourselves.

This is a poem for those
finally entering
the vacancies in their childhood
where love never stayed,

for those
healing the trauma
of any ideology
that siphoned light
from your eyes,

for those healing
the distorted myths
that there are parts of our nature
that must be reviled.

This is for those
healing the trauma
that our voices must
be swallowed,

that our feelings
must be reformed
until they look
like our family's comforts.

This is a poem for those
healing the million ways we've been told
love will leave us,

for those healing the need
to tiptoe
around infected secrets,

for those deliberately unlearning
the fragility
of feeling they could break
their family with a truth.

This is for the warriors
whose hearts,
unwilling to re-wound,
have become willing to weep.

NO FINER TRANSLATION

Grief removes weight
from our wings,

it clears out
the heavy boxes
from our past,

it untangles our knowing.

It's a rite of passage
that introduces you
to the custom-made gifts
awaiting you
in the unknown.

Grief is not pure sadness—
it is the brave and beautiful disarmament
of the soul.

It is the ecstasy of the heart's homecoming,

it's a plunge into the sea of oneness
that lives within us.

In grief, the human soul
can make no finer translation
of God's mighty song.

EVERYTHING AT ONCE

There are times
you grieve everything at once—
your childhood, your partner,
every bit
of your old God,

Your mortality,
your fleeting form,
the pain of your small grasp
on how to deeply and lastingly
love,

All the times
you made safe bets
with life
pretending you knew
what would come,

Your every trick
for controlling the Unknown
and putting God
in a headlock.

There are times you grieve
everything at once—

The time of the end
and the time of the beginning
are both soluble
in these tears.

And as you purge
this paradigm
of knowing only
your partial self,

Know that each loss is a death
and each death a wedding,
as we simultaneously break up
with the old relationship
to ourself

And wed truer versions
of the ravishing bride
of the eternal heart.

THE CLIMAX

An ecstatic poem
is the climax

From the conjugal visit
between the wildly divine
and achingly human

In the bed chambers
of the chest.

BREAKDOWN IN HEAVEN

Things were breaking down
in heaven.

There were fissures
in paradise.

And it was becoming harder and harder
for God to maintain His good image.

He had repressed His vulnerabilities
to the fiery rejection of hell
and His self-judgement was starting
to take him down.

For eternities God had worked
to bypass His hells
and scapegoat The Devil,
gaslighting Him for His anger
and such.

God abided in the dissociated
self-importance
of living in the clouds—
and getting His ass kissed
by white angels.

But it wasn't working so well anymore.

Those in hell
had begun rallying for their worth
and original innocence

Some of the celestial angels
were becoming swayed by this cause,
and the rebellious ones had altogether
let go of keeping the peace.
They joined the rally in The Underworld
protesting against the Narcissist Cult Leader
In The Sky.

And it didn't end there!
Heresy of heresies,
people had started calling God's gender into question
even going so far
as to call Him Her!!
He smote most of those hippies
but was running out
of lightning bolts.

The Lord entered a mood
of such high-level,
violent entitlement one day,
that even Angel Gabriel
became so emboldened
as to suggest to God
that it might be good for Him
to explore His feminine side!

The Time of The End
really accelerated though,
when The Devil finally gave up
His old strategy
of demanding salvation from God.
He stopped seeking revenge
or redemption
and just started accepting Himself.

Trying out creative agency,
The Devil even had plans
to create a community garden
in the center of hell.
And he started hosting
very popular workshops
about honoring your shadows!

Long story short,
all this eventually
brought God to His knees
and, bit by bit,
He grieved through His hells
of separation
and finally, disarmed of moral superiority,
came to ask the Devil
for forgiveness.

BAD INFLUENCE

The moon
is a shady character,
a bad influence

going around
promoting wildness
and freedom,
and making howling wolves
out of righteous,
God-fearing citizens.

She's been known to coerce
the proper and prim
to leave their well-trimmed yards,
as she leads them
into the dark forests
of themselves.

She throws the rule books
of stale, religious rhetoric
into the fire
and pulls some inner cork,
invoking in people a madness
to imbibe God.

Whatever you do,
do not listen
to the moon.

The moon is a heretic,
a wild-woman,
the feminist
in the sky.

She is intimate
with her darkness
and her light never trembles.

ARE YOU SIMPLY A VEHICLE?

I am a vehicle for poetry
because I have shed
a million skins.

I am a vehicle
because I have
time and time again
thrown comfort
into truth's fire.

My daily regimen
is putting my heart forward
even if the world
is not ready for it.

I try to eat a steady diet
of sunshine
and pique my thirst
for beauty.

I don't stop digging
for the God that lives
inside every pain,
and I know old demons
are just those
that have been waiting
to be alchemized
into wisdom.

I have made familiars
of chaos, terror
and the great mess
of life
that there may be
no energy that lives within me
from which I must scurry away.

I am a vehicle
because I care to live
no half-life.

DON'T ROMANTICIZE MY POETRY

Don't romanticize
my poetry—
my suffering
is my ink.

But neither defame me
for this confession—
for my suffering
is also the shimmering surface
of limitless wisdom.

Don't elevate me—
mysticism is born
from diving in to the mysteries
within the holy land
of each wound.

But do not degrade me—
for I have found God here.

QUIT

Quit
the marriage
that's still hurting you
in a patterned way
after you've done everything
to try and help it
heal.

Quit
the project
that takes more than it gives
and leads you to depletion.

Quit
the role
that makes you
reject yourself
to make someone else
comfortable.

Quit
the religion
that practices fear
instead of joy.

Quit
this thinking you must stay
to be worthy,
that you must stay
to be strong.

Not quitting can be great too,
at certain times,
but we already know that.

Sometimes to quit
is the bravest,
most loving thing
you could ever
do.

CRESCENT MOON

You see how the light
of the crescent moon
is such a tender cradle
for her darkness.

Oh, you too
can grow into
holding your shadows
like that.

GOD DID IT

The light of God
is the only revolutionary.

It's the light in each other
that's been too bright to see.
To look at it directly
would burn down
our separation.

It's the light
that overthrows
hierarchy.

It tosses your small identity
into the sea that cannot be separated
from all.

As Her revolution builds
in our hearts,
humanity evolves.

She is the Great Subversive One
who will speak up
for that which is true
even amidst those armed
with the harshest dedication
to falsehoods.

She is the lead abolitionist.

She is at the front
of feminist marches,

She is the origin
of any cause
that brings consciousness
forward.

If any religious dogmatists
or puffed-up men
get mad at me
for the great mercy
of my disruptive poetry—
She has told me
to use Her
as my scapegoat.

So I look at them
unflichingly
with a wry smile
and say,

"Don't blame me.
God did it."

SIT-INS

God stages sit-ins
in your body
on a regular basis—

it's very inconvenient
to law and order.

She says,
"Every time
there's even a micro-judgement,
an othering, a subjugation,
a hierarchical belittlement,
a domination
I sit. And stay."

We beg Her to be reasonable,

"Get over it, God!
These infractions happened
in the past. You're too sensitive.
Grow up.
Let bygones be bygones."

"Nope."
She says, in that unshakably
subversive way of Hers.

"Until you find a framework
of profound care, respect
and reverence
for those who have been

systematically wounded
by arrogance
I will not give up my protest
in you.

Your happiness
will have to be detoured,
your life force
held up,
your wisdom stalled,
your progress stunted
until it becomes such an inner upset
that you have to give these matters
attention.

I am The Great Nuisance,
The Insatiable Menace,
The Radical One.
I am The Crazy Bitch,
Society's Holy Wreckage.
I am She Who "Must Have Anger Problems,"
She Who "Can't Just Get Over It,"
and She Who "Must "Be Coming
From Victim Consciousness,"
for caring all the way
to the core
about the plight
of the disenfranchised
and about your liberation
from idiocy.

Call Me what you will,
but I promise
that until I become so miserable
to contend with

that you finally become brave enough
to change,
I ain't moving."

THE SEED OF MY HEART

I feel God
germinating the seed
of my heart
again

new life bursting
out through me

breaking down
all that I've known

that She may have more space
to love the world
through me.

GREAT MIRAGE

That your heart
is a small, beating, mortal thing
is really a great mirage,

An incredible sleight of hand!

Inside you'll find
an unfolding landscape
of God—

Moons and mountains
and a limitless
Love

That could never be bound
by anything so small
as death.

NO THERAPY QUITE COMPARES

There is no therapy
that quite compares
to immersing yourself
in nature,

To witness the nightly bloom
of the rose-gold moon,

To let the friction
of the crickets' song
re-spark your heart,

To sleep under the stars,
that luminous blueprint
of how little we know
of the reality
of God,

And let something of the universe
begins to hum in you again.

Curiosity
is generous enough
to find us here
as we begin again
to become enlivened
with the unanswerable.

Be near
unto a clear mountain stream
and a sacred element in the heart
becomes clarified.

Recline into the woods
and intentionally do nothing
but ask the intelligent hands
of Life
to unspin us of all
that isn't Her oneness.

The outdoors isn't native land
for man-made pressures.

Worries don't know
how to sustain themselves
in this territory.

The forest is represented
by the greatest diplomat,
Holy Silence,

who shows us something
of our mortality,
and that there's nothing
to fear of it.

SOMETHING OF THE MOUNTAINS

When I die, dear God,
please let me take something
of the mountains with me.

May I stow away,
inside a cavern of myself,
a glow from the moon?

Let me fill
any pockets my soul might have
with bits of silver rivers
and quiet starlight.

Can I pack a bag before I go
and bring only sunrise?

How many songs may I take?

Can I bring
the forest's exhale
after the rain?

Though my wildest imagination
cannot believe anything
could be better
than bare feet
pressed into dew-drenched grass
on this utterly love-soaked earth,

Tell me somehow
my passage
into the Beyond
will only widen my access
to beauty.

THE GREAT ART OF LOSS

The depth of my ability
to love
reveals the depth of my ability
to lose.

To lose is love's
inevitability
but our choice lies
in how beautifully
we lose.

In this great art of loss,
that is love,
our hearts are called
to unforeseen depths of courage.

To stand at the base
of love's great mountain
is to enter into a profound consultation
with the truth in our hearts

about what we're willing
to lay down of ourselves
on love's path.

If we are willing to lose
for love,
the eternal is grown
no matter what
becomes dust.

THE CLOUDS TOO

Like a heavy sky
that will never discontinue
being filled with the weighty blessings
of rain, my heart

Opens again to pour
in a way that enlivens all the earth
in its great, surrendered release
of sorrow.

And as the sunshine of remembrance
spreads its wide, golden arms
in my chest again,
it becomes clear—
the clouds too
were God.

QUIVERING BIRD

At least daily,
approach gently

the quivering bird
of your heart

and whisper,
"I'll never leave you."

APPROACH THIRSTY

Lately I've been praying to Muhammad,
Moses, Krishna, Buddha, Baha'u'llah, Zoroaster, Jesus—
why be choosy?

I ask any source of true love
and great joy
to throw me as many bones
as they might.

Sometimes I pray to Mozart, Bach or Galileo
to pour music or the stars
through me.

Often I pray to Tahirih,
a great Persian poet and feminist
of the 1800's who would remove
her veil when addressing men
and was martyred
for speaking the irrepressible truth
in her heart.

Her final words were,
"You can kill me as soon as you like,
but you will never stop
the emancipation of women."

I often ask Hafez for a dance
and we go for the most poetic whirls.

Sometimes I ask Rumi
that he pluck me an ancient,
everblooming rose
and I crush its scent
onto the page.

I have a crush on Kahlil Gibran
and ask that he pass me
inspired love notes.

I pray to Harriet Tubman,
that queen of heroism,
for courage
and to Einstein
for out of this world
ideas.

Inspiration is not elitist.
There is no muse
that is off limits,
no genius you should not approach
and ask to be yours.

Oh, beseech whoever you might
that the master keys
that open all hearts
are put in your care,
that your particularly necessary
style of expression
may open new portals of beauty
to the eyes of the world.

Hobnob with all the great
dead poets,
thinkers,
lovers,

artists,
heroes of justice,
leaders of truth.

They still want a place
to pour their wonder
into the world,
and you are a worthy vessel.

It's an open bar in the sky.
Approach thirsty,
and ask!

THE HOLY ONE

May each of us have a ceremony
as often as the reminder
is needed

for community to gather around us
and witness

a grandmother,
or a child,
or simply the clouds
that water spring,

anoint our brow,
sprinkle our head
with water's kiss of devotion,
and whisper in our ear—

*"We acknowledge the holy one
you've always been."*

Printed in the USA
CPSIA information can be obtained
at www.ICGtesting.com
JSHW022255080424
60798JS00001B/36

9 781958 972120